About the Author

Mrs. Jyoti Giramkar has 10 years of experience in Excel Macros. She has worked on many excel VBA Projects

Her hobbies are travelling to new tourist places, watching football, cricket and learning latest technological stuff.

A special note of Thanks to My Husband

I would like to dedicate this book to my lovely husband for loving me so much and helping me write this book. Without his support, this book would not have been a reality.

Preface

This book covers all topics on excel macro. Excel is widely used across world. Knowing excel macro is always a step forward in one's skillsets.

Major topics covered in this book are.

1. Introduction to Excel Macros
2. VBA Editor
3. VBA Programming Basics
4. Writing and running macros
5. Automating workbook tasks
6. Automating worksheet tasks
7. Automating daily excel tasks
8. Working with pivot table and charts.

Table of Contents

1. Excel Macro Introduction

1.1. Why we need Excel Macros

Excel Macro is nothing but a computer program written in VBA programming language in Excel visual Basic Editor.

I am happy that you have decided to learn excel macros. Excel macros are very important as they can really help you to perform the repeatative tasks automatically.

Advantages of the Excel Macro –

1. Automate the daily repeatative tasks in Excel.
2. Saves time and effort.
3. Write once and use many times.
4. Send an automated email.
5. Perform the analysis on the data automatically.
6. Easy to use.

As I mentioned earlier, macro is a computer program. So we can perform any task based upon the logic we use in the code. So there are unlimited advantages of the excel macro.

But sometimes, macro could be disasterous if it contains malicious code. So we should be very careful when opening the excel workbook containing macros.I will advise you to not open any macro workbook from untrusted source.

1.2. Applications of Excel Macros

As I said earlier, Excel macro is just like any other software program. So if you can use good logic, macro could be very helpful.

Below is the sample list of most commonly used applications of Excel Macros.

1. Filter the data from worksheet.
2. Sort the data from worksheet.
3. Send a workbook as an email.
4. Create pivot table and pivot chart for data analysis.
5. Create new workbooks and save them.
6. Move data from one workbook to another.
7. Process and analyse the data based on the business conditions.
8. Group the data based some filters.

2. Basics of Excel Macro

In this chapter you will learn about below topics.

1. Visual basic editor features in Excel.
2. Record new macro
3. Debug a macro
4. Run a Macro.
5. Basic VBA programming
6. Modules
7. Sub procedures
8. Functions.

2.1 Recording excel macros

Before I tell you how to record macros, let me explain how to show developer Tab in Excel 2010.

On the menubar, you have to right click and then you will see below context menu. Click on Customize the ribbon.

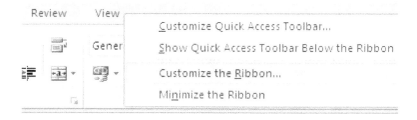

Figure 1 - Customize Ribbon

After this, you will see ribbon dialog window. It will show the main tabs as displayed in below figure. You have to select the checkbox in front of the Developer tab and then click on Ok

Figure 2 - Select Developer Tab

After you click on ok button, developer tab will be shown in Excel menu bar as shown in below figure.

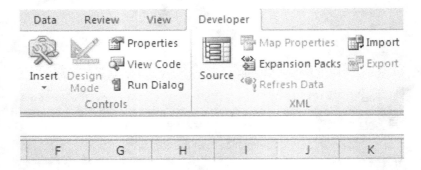

Figure 3 - Developer Tab

When you click on the developer tab, you will see below command group at the left side. To record a new macro , you will have to click on – "Record Macro" command button.

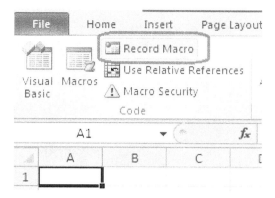

Figure 4 - Record Macro Button

Next below dialog window will open asking you the details of the macro you will be recording

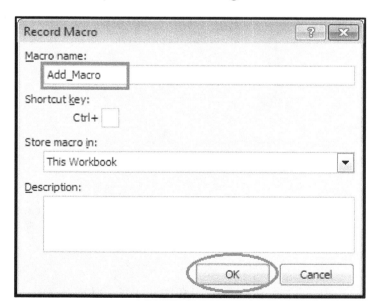

You will have to provide the name of macro. You can also assign the shortcut key to macro. You can store the macro in current workbook or any other workbook as well. Finally

you have to give the description of the macro. Please note that your macro name should not contain blank spaces and other special characters like $#@!

After you click on the ok button, macro recording starts. Whatever operation you do on excel sheet will be recorded and macro code will be created automatically.

For the simplicity, I am going to perform addition of values in the cells A3 and B3. The sum of these 2 values will be stored in the cell - C3 as displayed in below figure. But if you want, you can perform any complex calaculations while recording. You can even add charts as well.

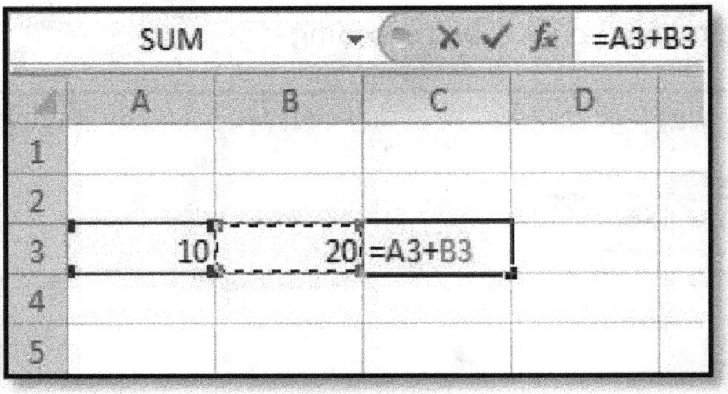

Figure 5 - Recording Macro

After this you can stop recording the macro by clicking on the button displayed in the developer tab as shown in below figure.

That's all. You have just created new macro in excel.

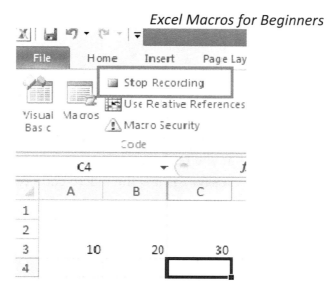

Figure 6 - Stop recording

2.2 View and Run excel macro.

You can view excel macro by clicking the macros button displayed near record button.

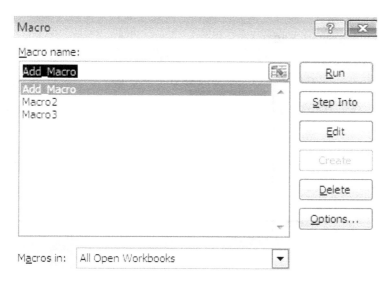

Figure 7 - View Macros

As shown in above figure, You will be able to see all macros in open workbooks. On the right hand side, you will be able to see buttons to run, debug, edit, delete buttons. To run the macro, just click on the Run button. All operations that you performed while recording will be done automatically. To view the macro code you can click on edit button.

3.3 Debugging the excel macro.

When you click on the edit button in previuos window, you will see the macro code as shown in below figure. You can debug the code to see how the macro performs each operation in sequence. You can also find the errors in the macro by debugging it.

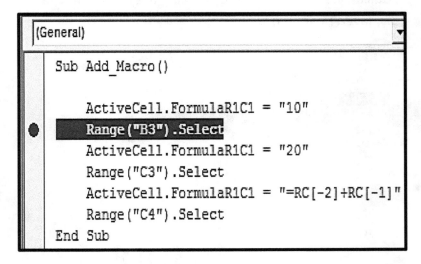

Figure 8 - Debug the macro

To add breakpoint, you have to click on the vertical bar in front of the line of code. When you run the macro, control will pause at the breakpoint and from there you can execute your code line by line using F8 key.

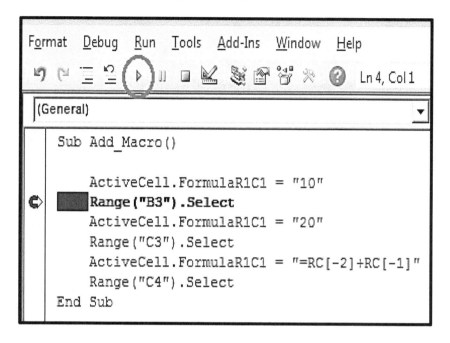

Figure 9 - Macro control pauses at breakpoint

3.4 Visual Basic Editor

You can open visual basic editor by clicking on the visual basic command button as shown in below figure.

Figure 10 – Open Visual Basic Editor

Visual basic editor window will show you excel sheet objects, modules and macros in the workbook as shown in below figure.

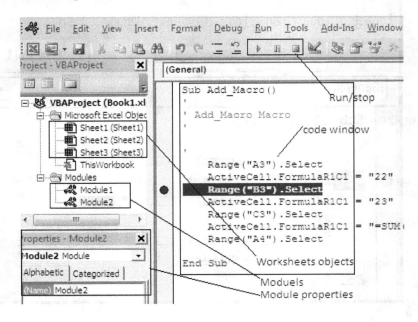

Figure 11 - VB Editor in Excel

We have below windows in VBA Editor that can be used while running macro.

1. Watch Window
2. Immediate Window
3. Locals Window

These 3 windows help us in debugging the macro. In watch window, we can inspect the variables value.

Let us have a look at each window.

Watch Window

To see the value of the variable, in the debug mode you have to right click on it and then select add to watch. As seen in next figure, I have added variable a to the watch window and the value of a is 20 .

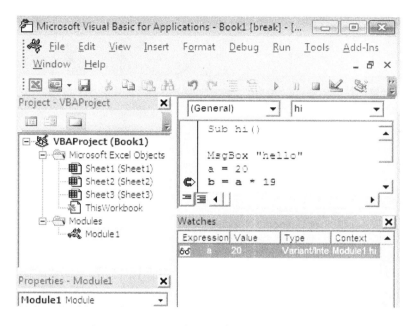

Figure 12 - Watch Window in VBA Editor

Immediate Window

We can use immediate window to see the output of the macro as shown in next figure. The debug.print statement will print the value |23 in the immediate window. This is how we can monitor if our program is producing correct output or not.

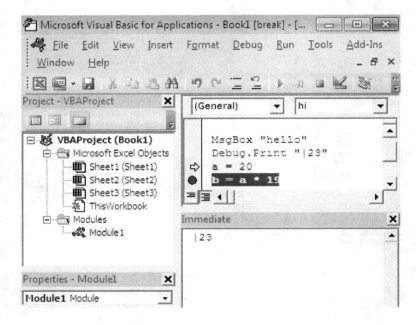

Figure 13 - Immediate Window in VBA Editor

Locals Window

We can use Locals window to see the values of local variables. As shown in next figure, we have a locals window showing the values of variables a and b. Locals window is also showing the data type of these variables.

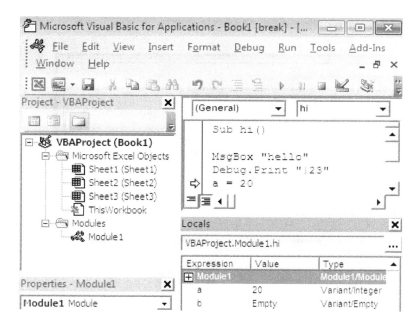

Figure 14 - Locals Window in VBA Editor

3.5 Modules in VBA

Modules are used to store the macros together. We can group similar macros in a separate module for easy reference.

Actually when you record a macro, that macro code is stored in the modules.

3.6 Sub routines in VBA

Sub routines are nothing but macro procedures. They are used to increase the reusability of the code. You can call the same sub procedure any number of time to perform specific task.

For example in below figure, there is one macro or sub procedure called Add_Macro.

```
(General)

    Sub Add_Macro ()

    Set WB = Workbooks.Add
     WB.Title = "New WB"
     WB.SaveAs Filename:="D:\F1.xls"

    End Sub
```

3.7 Functions in VBA

Functions are similar to the sub procedures. Only the difference is that functions return a value while procedure does not return a value.

Function Example

In below example, I have created one function called add which takes 2 input values a and b. Then it adds 2 numbers and returns the sum to calling sub – sample.

```
Sub sample()

    x = add(2, 3)
    MsgBox x

End Sub

Function add(a, b)

    add = a + b

End Function
```

3.8 User Forms in VBA

VBA editor also provides the feature called user forms which can be used to create the interactive user forms.

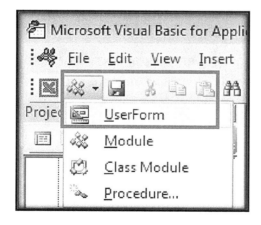

Figure 15 - User Forms in VBA

When you add user form to the VBA project, you will see new user form in design mode. You will also see the toolbox showing common form controls like command button, checkbox, radiobutton, textbox, combobox etc.

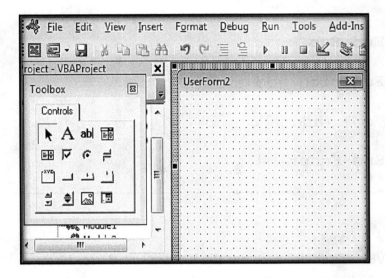

You can create windows based applications using user forms. For example – You can add command button in the form and then call a macro on button click event.

3.9 Events in VBA

VBA is an event driven programming language. All important excel objects like worksheets and workbooks support events.

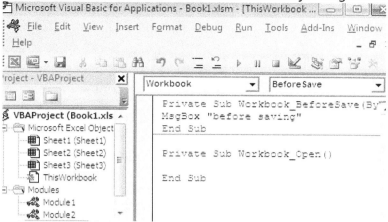

When you double click on the worksheet or workbook object you can see what all events that object support.

For example – As shown in previous figure, you can see events supported by workbook. Second combobox contains all events. When you select new event from the dropdown, the code for that event is automatically added in the code window.

In below code, I have added code which will execute when you try to save the current workbook.

```
Private Sub Workbook_BeforeSave(ByVal
SaveAsUI As Boolean, Cancel As Boolean)

        MsgBox "before saving"

End Sub
```

3. Excel Macro Settings

In this chapter, you will learn below topics.

1. How to save the excel workbook containing macros
2. How to enable /disable macros
3. Understand Trust Center settings
4. Adding macro commands to toolbar

3.1 Saving excel macro workbooks

In Microsoft Excel 2010, when you add macro to workbook, you will have to save that workbook with **xlsm** extension. If you try to save the workbook with other extension, you will get below error.

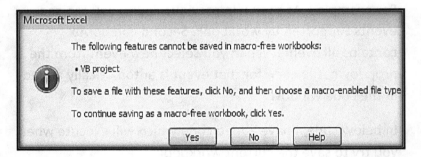

3.2 Enabling excel macro.

When you try to open excel workbook which contains macros, you may see below message saying that macros may contain viruses or other securtiy hazards. Do not enable this content unless you trust th esource of this file.

You will also see 2 buttons – enable macros and disable macros. If you know the source of the excel file and you really want to use macros, then only you should click on enable macros button. Otherwise it is good practise to click on disable macros.

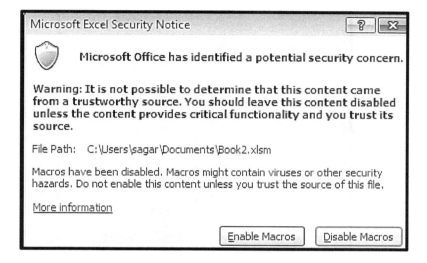

3.3 Understanding Trust Center settings

Trust Center provides important settings related to macros. To open trust center you will have to follow below steps.

1. Click on options in File Menu.
2. In Excel options window, click on Trust Center.
3. There you will have to click on Trust Center settings button.
4. Trust Center window Opens.

As you can see in next figure, trust center has important settings related to the macro like

1. Trusted Publishers.
2. Trusted Locations.

3. Trusted Documents.
4. Macro Settings

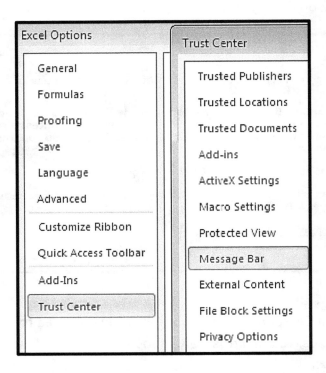

Figure 16 - Trust Center Settings

3.4 Adding Macros to the toolbar

As I said earlier,we can execute the macros by going to developer tab and then clicking on macros buttons, you will see all macros.

You can also run the macro by adding a command to toolbar. You will have to follow below steps to creat a macro command button.

1. Open a cutomize ribbon window.
2. From left side drop down, select macros option

3. Create a custom command group.
4. Add macro that you want to show on toolbar.

Below figure shows how we can do it.

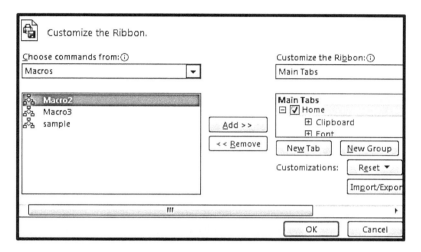

Figure 17 - Adding the macro to toolbar

Figure 18 - Macro added to toolbar

As you can see in above figure, I have added macro 3 to the custom command group in Home tab. You can execute that macro by just clicking on it.

4. VBA(Macro) Programming Concepts

This is the most important chapter. In this chapter, you will learn basic concepts in VBA language like….

4.1 Variables and data types in VBA

Variables are used to store the data in the program. It is not mandatory to declare the variables in VBA. The data type of the variable changes as per the type of data we store in that variable.

<u>Variables Declaration</u>
Syntax:-
         Dim VariableName As Data Type
For Example

```
Dim no As Integer
Dim str1 As String
Dim c As Characters
```

<u>Variables initialization</u>

```
Dim str As String
str = "String name"
```

Variables are of 2 types.
1. Scalar – stores one value at a time
2. Array – stores multiple values at a time

VBA has mainly 2 types of Data Types – numeric and non-numeric..

1. Numeric
2. Non - Numeric

Numeric Data Types

Type	Storage	Range of Values
Byte	1 Byte	0 to 255
Integer	2 bytes	-32,768 to 32,767
Long	4 bytes	-2,147,483,648 to 2,147,483,648
Single	4 bytes	-3.402823E+38 to -1.401298E-45 for negative values 1.401298E-45 to 3.402823E+38 for positive values.
Double	8 bytes	-1.79769313486232e+308 to -4.94065645841247E-324 for negative values 4.94065645841247E-324 to 1.79769313486232e+308 for positive values.
Currency	8 bytes	-922,337,203,685,477.5808 to 922,337,203,685,477.5807
Decimal	12 bytes	+/- 79,228,162,514,264,337,593,543,950,335 if no decimal is use +/- 7.9228162514264337593543950335 (28 decimal places)

Non-Numeric Data Types

Data Type	Storage	Range
String(fixed length)	Length of string	1 to 65,400 characters
String(variable length	Length + 10 bytes	0 to 2 billion characters
Date	8 bytes	January 1, 100 to December 31, 9999

Boolean	2 bytes	True or False
Object	4 bytes	Any embedded objec
Variant(numeric	16 bytes	Any value as large as Double
Variant(text)	Length+22 bytes	Same as variable-length string

4.2 Control statements (Conditional and loop)

VBA has 2 kinds of conditional statements.

1. If ..then ..else
2. Select ...case

1) If...Then ...Else

```
Sub condition()
    Dim a As Integer
    Dim b As Integer
     a = 10
     b = 15
  If (a > b) Then
     MsgBox "a is grater"
  Else
     MsgBox "b is grater"

  End If

End Sub
```

2) Select case

```
Sub Selectcase()
    Dim a As Integer
    Dim b As Integer
    Dim c As Integer

        a = 10
        b = 15

    Select Case (3)
      Case 1
         c = a + b
         MsgBox (c)
      Case 2
         c = a - b
         MsgBox (c)
      Case 3
         c = a * b
         MsgBox (c)
    End Select

End Sub
```

VBA has 2 kinds of loop statements.
1. Do While..loop
2. For loop

3) Do While...Loop

```
Sub Whileloop()
```

```
    Dim i As Integer
    i = 1
    Dim str As String
       str = "Computer"
    Do While i <= 10

        Cells(i, 2).Value = str
         i = i + 1
    Loop

End Sub
```

Output:

	A	B	C
1		Computer	
2		Computer	
3		Computer	
4		Computer	
5		Computer	
6		Computer	
7		Computer	
8		Computer	
9		Computer	
10		Computer	
11			

4) For....Next loop

```
Sub Forloop()

    Dim i As Integer

    For i = 1 To 10
```

```
      Cells(i, 1).Value = i
   Next

End Sub
```

Output:

B2	▼	⊕

◢	A	B	C
1	1		
2	2		
3	3		
4	4		
5	5		
6	6		
7	7		
8	8		
9	9		
10	10		
11			

4.3 String functions in VBA

String functions are used to perform various operations on the text values in VBA. Below example will demonstrate all string function in VBA.

```
Sub Stringfunction()

   Dim str As String

   'to get the position of a substring
```

```
Cells(1, 1).Value = "sagar salunke "
    str = Cells(1, 1).Value
    Cells(3, 2) = InStr(str, "p")

    'to extract substring from the left
    Cells(4, 2) = Left(str, 4)

    'to extract substring from the right
    Cells(5, 2) = Right(str, 5)

    'to get the middle part of string
    Cells(6, 2) = Mid(str, 3, 7)

    'to get the length of a string
    str = Cells(1, 1).Value
    Cells(7, 2) = Len(str)

    'to Convert the string to lower case
    Cells(8, 2) = LCase(str)

    'to Convert the string to upper
    Cells(9, 2) = UCase(str)

    'to trim the string
    Cells(10, 2) = Trim(str)

    'to trim the string from left

    Cells(11, 2) = LTrim(str)

    'to trim the string from right

    Cells(12, 2) = RTrim(str)

    'to Replace the string

    Cells(13, 2) = Replace("This is a ",
"a", "computer")
```

```
'to Reverse the string
str = Cells(1, 1).Value
Cells(14, 2) = StrReverse(str)



'to Compare two strings
Cells(16, 2) = StrComp(str, "macro")

End Sub
```

	A	B
1	sagar salunke	
2		
3	instr	0
4	left	saga
5	right	unke
6	mid	gar sal
7	length	14
8	lcase	sagar salunke
9	ucase	SAGAR SALUNKE
10	trim	sagar salunke
11	ltrim	sagar salunke
12	rtrim	sagar salunke
13	replace	This is computer
14	reverse	eknulas ragas

Figure 19 - String Function Output

34

4.4 Date and Time functions in VBA

We can perform date and time operations easily using below functions

1. Now – gets current system timestamp
2. Date – gets current system date
3. DateAdd – adds interval to date
4. DateDiff – finds the difference between 2 dates.

1)DateAdd Example

Syntax:- DateAdd(interval,number,date)

The interval you want to add

- yyyy -Year
- q -Quarter
- m -Month
- y - Day of year
- d -Day
- w -Weekday
- ww - Week of year
- h -Hour
- n -Minute
- s –Second

```
Sub Addatefunction()

    'return the current date and time
    Cells(3, 2) = Now

    'Return the current date
    Cells(4, 2) = Date
```

```
    'Add Year
    Cells(4,2)=(DateAdd("yyyy",2,Date))

    'Add Month
    Cells(5, 2)=(DateAdd("m", 2, Date))

    'Add day
    Cells(6, 2)=(DateAdd("d", 2, Date))

    'Add Weekday
    Cells(7, 2)=(DateAdd("w", 8, Date))

    'Add Week of year
    Cells(8, 2)=(DateAdd("ww", 2, Date))

    'Add Hours
    Cells(9, 2) = (DateAdd("h", 1, Now))

    'Add Minutes
    Cells(10,2)=(DateAdd("n",1 Now))

    'Add Seconds
    Cells(11, 2) = (DateAdd("s",1,Now))


End Sub
```

2) DateDiff Example

```
Sub Datedifffunction()

firstDate = "11-Mar-14 00:00:00"
secondDate = "31-Mar-15 23:59:00"
```

```
Cells(3,2)=CStr(DateDiff("yyyy",
fDate,tDate))
Cells(4, 2) = (DateDiff("q", firstDate,
secondDate))

Cells(5, 2) = (DateDiff("m", firstDate,
secondDate))

Cells(6, 2) = (DateDiff("h", firstDate,
secondDate))

Cells(7, 2) = (DateDiff("w", firstDate,
secondDate))

Cells(8, 2) = (DateDiff("s", firstDate,
secondDate))

Cells(9, 2) = (DateDiff("ww", firstDate,
secondDate))

Cells(10, 2) = (DateDiff("y", firstDate,
secondDate))

Cells(11, 2) = (DateDiff("d", firstDate,
secondDate))

Cells(12, 2) = (DateDiff("n", firstDate,
secondDate))

End Sub
```

Output:-

	A	B	C
1			
2	**Difference**		
3	Year	1	
4	Quarter	4	
5	Months	12	
6	Hour	9263	
7	Weekday	55	
8	Second	33350340	
9	Week of y	55	
10	Day of yea	385	
11	Day	385	
12	Minute	555839	
13			

Figure 20-Datediff

3) DatePart

```
Sub Datepartfunction()

    'return the date
    d = CDate("2010-02-16")
    Cells(3, 2) = (DatePart("d", d))

     'Return month
    d = CDate("2010-02-16")
    Cells(4, 2) = (DatePart("m", d))

     'Return Year
    d = CDate("2010-02-16")
    Cells(5, 2) = (DatePart("yyyy", d))
```

```
    'Return Hours
   Cells(6, 2) = (DatePart("h", Now()))

    'Return Minutes
   Cells(7, 2) = (DatePart("n", Now()))

    'Return Seconds
   Cells(8, 2) = (DatePart("s", Now()))

End Sub
```

Output :-

	A	B	C
1			
2	**DatePart is**		
3	Date	16	
4	Month	2	
5	Year	2010	
6	Hours	17	
7	Minutes	3	
8	Seconds	53	
9			
10			

4) DateSerial

Syntax:- DateSerial(year,month,day)

```
Sub Dateserialfunction()
```

```
Cells(3,2)=CDate(DateSerial(2014,3,27))

    'Subtract 15 days:
  Cells(4,2)=(DateSerial(2014,3,6-15))

    'Add 5 Days
  Cells(5,2)=(DateSerial(2014,3,6+5))

End Sub
```

Output:-

▲	A	B	C
1			
2		DateSerial	
3	Print serial	27-03-2014	
4	Subtract 15 days	19-02-2014	
5	Add 5 days	11-03-2014	
6			
7			
8			
9			

5) DateValue

```
Sub Datevaluefunction()

   Cells(8,2)=(DateValue("27-Mar-14"))

End Sub
```

Output:-

◢	A	B	C
1			
2		**Date Value**	
3		27-03-2014	
4			
5			
6			

6) FormatDateTime

```
Sub Formatdatefun()

    Cells(3,2)=(FormatDateTime(Now()))
    Cells(4,2)=(FormatDateTime(Now(),1))
    Cells(5,2)=(FormatDateTime(Now(),2))
    Cells(6,2)=(FormatDateTime(Now(),3))
    Cells(7,2)=(FormatDateTime(Now(),4))

End Sub
```

Output :-

	A	B	C
1			
2	**Format date time**		
3	Current datetim	27-03-2014 17:24:38	
4	Long date	27-Mar-14	
5	Short date	27-03-2014	
6	long time	17:24:38	
7	short time	17:24	
8			
9			

7) IsDate

IsDate function returns the True Or False

```
Sub Isdatefun()

    Cells(3,2)=(IsDate("April 22,1947"))

    Cells(6,2)=(IsDate("52/17/2010"))

    Cells(4,2)=(IsDate(#1/31/2010#))

    Cells(5,2)=(IsDate("#01/31/10#"))

End Sub
```

Output :-

⯆	A	B
1		
2		**IsDate**
3		TRUE
4		TRUE
5		FALSE
6		FALSE
7		
8		
9		

8) WeekdayName

```
Sub Weekdayfun()

    Cells(3, 2) = (WeekdayName(5))

End Sub
```

4.5 Math functions in VBA

Important Math functions in VBA are given below.

1. Round – finds the round value of the number
2. Abs – finds the absolute value
3. Sqrt – finds square root of the number
4. ^ - finds x^y

```
Sub Weekdayfun()

  x = 2 ^ 3
    MsgBox x
```

```
    'prints 8

    MsgBox Round(33.243, 2)
    'prints 33.24

    MsgBox Abs(-23.22)
    'prints 23.22

    MsgBox Sqr(4)
    'prints 2

    MsgBox (Exp(5.5))
    'print 244.69193226422

    MsgBox (Int(4.4567))
    'print 4

    MsgBox (Tan(55))
    'print -45.1830879105211

    MsgBox (Rnd)
    'print 0.5795186

End Sub
```

4.6 Excel object model in VBA

Excel Application is built using object oreinted programming paradigm. So everything is object in Excel. . To view all objects in Excel you can click on object browser button in VBA as shown in below figure

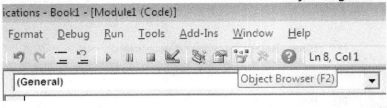

Figure 21 - Click on the Object Browser Button

Figure 22 - View Excel library Objects

Then you can select Excel library from the dropdown to view all objects as shown in the above figure. To return to code window, you will have to press F7.

List of important objects and collections in Excel is given below.

1. Application
2. Workbook
3. Worksheet
4. Range
5. Workbooks
6. Worksheets
7. Shape
8. Chart
9. Font
10. Border
11. Comment

5. Automating Workbooks using macros.

In this chapter you will learn about automating the workbook tasks using macros like....

1.   Creating and saving new workbook
2.   Deleteing existing workbook
3.   Opening and reading a workbook
4.   Protecting workbook

5.1 Creating a new workbook

Below Code/Example can be used to create a new Excel workbook and save it using VBA Macro.

Syntax and Example of VBA Macro to Create a new workbook.

```
Sub AddNewWorkbook()

 Set WB = Workbooks.Add
 WB.Title = "New WB"
 WB.SaveAs Filename:="D:\F1.xls"

End Sub
```

Above code will create a new workbook with title as New WB and It will Save the new Workbook to location @ D:\F1.xls

5.2 Delete a workbook

We can use below macro code to delete a workbook. The first line in the code creates the file system object. Then we have used deletefile method to delete a workbook stored at d:\f1.xls.

```
Set fso =
CreateObject("scripting.filesystemobject
")

fso.deletefile ("d:\f1.xls")
```

5.3 Open a workbook

We can use below macro code to open a workbook. The first line in the code will open the workbook located at location d:\f1.xls. Then we have stored a value 22 in the cell A1. Then we have used save method and closed the workbook using close method

```
Sub Open_Workbook()

Set wb=
Application.Workbooks.Open("D:\F1.xls")

wb.ActiveSheet.Cells(1, 1) = "22"
wb.Save
wb.Close

End Sub
```

5.4 Protect a workbook

We can use below macro code to protect workbook.

```
ActiveWorkbook.protect Structure:=True,
Windows:=False
```

6. Automating Worksheets using Macros

In this chapter you will learn about automating the worksheet tasks using macros like....

1. Inserting a new worksheet
2. Hiding a worksheet
3. Unhiding a worksheet
4. Deleteing existing worksheet
5. Protecting worksheet
6. Rearranging the worksheets
7. Changing the colour of the worksheet tab
8. Copy worksheet from one workbook to another
9. Moving worksheet across workbooks.

6.1 Inserting new worksheet

Below Example Shows how we can create a new Worksheet using Macro.

In below code, we are trying to add new worksheet with name –"sagar" in current workbook. If the worksheet with name – "sagar" already exists, macro code will show pop up message saying the sheet already exists. If the sheet does not exist, new sheet will be added.

```
mySheet = "Sagar"
On Error Resume Next

Temp = Worksheets(mySheet).Name

If Err.Number = 0 Then
```

```
    MsgBox "The sheet already Exists "


Else

    Err.Clear
    Worksheets.Add.Name = mySheet
    MsgBox "The New sheet Created "

End if
```

This is how we can create a new worksheet using a VBA macro in Excel 2010/2003/2007.

6.2 Hide a worksheet
Below Example will hide a worksheet3.

```
Sheet3.Visible = False
```

6.3 Unhide a worksheet
Below Example will unhide a worksheet3.

```
Sheet3.Visible = True
```

6.4 Sort the worksheets in worksbook

Below Example will sort the worksheets in alphbetical order and then move them accordingly.

```
Mysheets= Sheets.Count

    For i = 1 To Mysheets- 1

        For j = i + 1 To Mysheets

If Sheets(j).Name < Sheets(i).Name Then
    Sheets(j).Move before:=Sheets(i)
    ' Swap the sheets
End If

        Next j

    Next i
```

Above code will sort the worksheets in Workbook using Excel Macro in 2007/2010/2003.

6.5 Move worksheets

Below macro code will move worksheet sagar from current workbook to another open workbook – Book1.xlsm

The last statement will determine the position where you have added a worksheet. In below code we have added the worksheet after sheet1.

Sheets("sagar").Select

```
Sheets("sagar").move
After:=Workbooks("Book1.xlsm").Sheets(1)
```

To move the sheet to same workbook, you will have below syntax.

```
Sheets("sagar").move After:=Sheets(1)
```

6.6 Copy worksheets

Below macro code will copy worksheet sheet4 from current workbook to another open workbook – Book1.xlsm

The last statement will determine the position where you have added a worksheet. In below code we have added the worksheet after sheet at index 1.

```
Sheets("Sheet4").Select
```

```
Sheets("Sheet4").Copy
Before:=Workbooks("Book1.xlsm").Sheets(1)
```

To copy the sheet to same workbook, you will have below syntax.

```
Sheets("Sheet4").Copy Before:=Sheets(1)
```

6.7 Delete worksheet from a workbook

Below macro code will delete the worksheet with name sheet1 from current workbook.

```
Application.DisplayAlerts = False
```

```
Sheets("Sheet1").Delete
```

Please note that we have set the DisplayAlerts property to false to suppres the dialog window. Otherwise You will encouter below warning message saying – data may exist in the sheet(s) selected for deletion. To permanently delete the data, Press Delete.

6.8 How to rename worksheet

If you want to change the name of existing worksheet, it is very simple to do in macro. Below code will rename the sheet3 to Sales.

Sheets("Sheet3").Select

Sheets("Sheet3").Name = "sales"

6.9 How to Change Tab color of worksheet

Below macro code will change the tab color of the sheet3.

Sheets("sales").Select

With ActiveWorkbook.Sheets("sales").Tab

.ThemeColor = xlThemeColorLight2

.TintAndShade = -0.249977111117893

End With

7. Manipulating data using Excel Macro

In this chapter you will learn about how you can process or analyse the data in the cell or range of cells using macros like....

1. Sorting data in a column
2. Filtering the data in a column
3. Protecting cells
4. Inserting and deleting the rows
5. Inserting and deleting the columns
6. Formatting the cells
7. Finding the blanks cells, rows and columns
8. Adding functions in the cells
9. Trim the cell values
10. Replacing the cell values
11. Copying rows, columns or range
12. Cutting the rows, columns or range

7.1 Inserting and deleting the rows

1) Insert rows and columns

Example - Below code will add a new column at B. Old data at column B will be shifted to right.

```
activeworksheet.Columns("B:B").Select
Selection.Insert
```

This is how we can add column at any position in excel using macro.

Example - Below code will add/ Insert blank row in Excel Sheet

Macro Code / Syntax to Add new Row in Excel.

```
Rows("6:6").Select
 Selection.Insert Shift:=xlDown,
CopyOrigin:=xlFormatFromLeftOrAbove
```

Above code will add / Insert new row at row number 6. Old row at row number 6 will be pushed down.

This is how we can add or insert new / Blank row in excel.

2)Delete existing rows and columns

```
activeworksheet.Columns("B:B").Select
Selection.Delete

activeworksheet.Rows("1:1").Select
Selection.Delete
```

3) Find blank rows and cells

Below Example will count all blank cells from given range in the worksheets

VBA Macro Code / Syntax :

```
n =
Range("h3:h30").Cells.SpecialCells(xlCel
lTypeBlanks).Count
MsgBox n          'Print all blank cells

Here xlCellTypeBlanks means that cell is
blank.


n =
Range("h3:h30").Cells.SpecialCells(xlCel
lTypeConstants).Count
MsgBox n        ' Print all cells with
constant values not formulas
```

This is how we can find out the blank cells in Excel Macro.

4) Select Entire Row/Column in Excel VBA Macro

Example - We can select entire row or column vey easily using below code.

Code and Syntax :

To Select Entire Row No 2 –

```
Workbooks("Book1").Sheets("Sheet1").Rang
e("2:2").Font.Bold = True
```

To Select Entire Column A –

```
Workbooks("Book1").Sheets("Sheet1").Ran
ge("A:A").Font.Bold = True
```

To Select Cell A1 -

```
Workbooks("Book1").Sheets("Sheet1").Rang
e("A1").Font.Bold = True
```

To Select Cell Range –

```
Workbooks("Book1").Sheets("Sheet1").Rang
e("A1:B8").Font.Bold = True
```

To Select Multiple Cell Range –

```
Workbooks("Book1").Sheets("Sheet1").Rang
e("A1:B8,G3:I9").Font.Bold = True
```

To Select Multiple Columns sequentially –

```
Workbooks("Book1").Sheets("Sheet1").Rang
e("A:C").Font.Bold = True
```

To Select Multiple Columns Not sequentially –

```
Workbooks("Book1").Sheets("Sheet1").Rang
e("A:A,C:C").Font.Bold = True
'Here Columns A and C will be selected.
```

5) Different Excel Cell Types in VBA Macros

Below is the list of All Cell Types in VBA Macros

xlCellTypeAllFormatConditions - Cells of any format
xlCellTypeAllValidation   - validation criteria Cells
xlCellTypeBlanks   - Empty /Blank cells
xlCellTypeComments   - Cells with comments
xlCellTypeConstants   - Cells with constants values
xlCellTypeFormulas   - Cells having formulas
xlCellTypeLastCell   - last cell in the used range
xlCellTypeSameFormatConditions - Cells having the same format
xlCellTypeSameValidation   - Cells having the same validation criteria
xlCellTypeVisible   - All visible cells

Example -

```
msgbox
Range("h3:h30").Cells.SpecialCells(xlCel
lTypeBlanks).Count
```

This will print the number of cells in given range that are of type - xlCellTypeBlanks. Means it will print the count of blank cells.

6) Clear contents of certain cells in Excel sheet

Example -

In below example I am going to show you how we can clear the contents of specified cells in excel sheet.
I will also show you how we can use macro to clear the contents of entire row or column.

Code and Syntax to clear the contents of specified cells using macro.

Code to clear the contents of certain cell.

```
 Range("A18").Select
 Selection.ClearContents
```

Code to clear the contents of multiple cells.

```
Range("A2:B22").Select
   ' clear contents of a range
Selection.ClearContents
```

Code to clear the contents of Entire row in Excelsheet

```
 rows("2:2").Select
```

```
Selection.ClearContents
```

Code to clear the contents of Entire Column in Excelsheet

```
columns("A:A").Select
Selection.ClearContents
```

In similar way we can clear the contents of any cells, ranges in excel sheet using VBA macro. It is just two step process.

- Select the area/region you want to clear.
- Use Selection.ClearContents statement.

7.2 Formatting the cells

1) Change the font color and size of Cell in Excel

Below example will change the font size as well as font color of text inside the cell in worksheet in Excel Workbook.

Code and Syntax

```
Activeworksheet.Range("A1").select

    Selection.Font.Italic = True
'make the font italic in macro
```

```
    Selection.Font.Bold = False
'make the font bold in macro

    Selection.Font.Underline =
xlUnderlineStyleSingle
'Underline the macro.

    Selection.Font.ThemeColor =
xlThemeColorLight2
' Change the color of cell

    Selection.Font.TintAndShade =
0.399975585192419
'Change the shade of color

    Selection.Font.Name = "Calibri"
'Change the name of font

    Selection.Font.Size = 20
'Change the size of macro

    Selection.Font.Strikethrough = False
'Other features of font like
strikethrough

    Selection.Font.Superscript = False
'Subscript, Shadow, Underline etc.

    Selection.Font.Subscript = False

    Selection.Font.OutlineFont = False

     Selection.Font.Shadow = False

    Selection.Font.Underline =
xlUnderlineStyleSingle

  Selection.Font.Color = -16776961
```

```
Selection.Font.TintAndShade = 0
```

2) Set the background color of cell using Excel VBA Macro

In below example, I have changed the background color of the A1 using a Macro.

Code / Syntax : -

```
Range("A1").Interior.ColorIndex = 8
 'Change the background color of Cell A1

Range("A1".EntireRow.Interior.ColorIndex
= 8
 'Change the background color of Entire
Row.
```

This is how we can change the background color of Cell/Range in Excel using VBA Macro

3) Changing data in cells relative to each other

We can enter data in the relative cells using offset property. In below example we have set the value 22 and set the font color of the cell to green which is placed at

2 rows down and 3 columns to the right of cell A1

```
Sub offset_property()

'Offset property is used to access the
cell in a relative manner

Worksheets(1).Cells(1, 1).Offset(2,
3).value = 22

Worksheets(1).Cells(1, 1).Offset(2,
3).Font.Color = vbGreen

End Sub
```

4) Change the font of multiple rows in excel macro

Below macro code illustrates how we can change the font of multiple rows.

```
Sub change_font_multiple_rows()

'We can select multiple rows using below
syntax

'For single row
'In below example we have changed the
font of the row number 1
Worksheets(1).Range("1:1").Font.Bold =
False


'For multiple sequential rows
```

```
'In below example we have changed the
font of all the rows from 1 to 4
Worksheets(1).Range("1:4").Font.Bold =
False

'For multiple non-sequential rows
Worksheets(1).Range("1:1,3:3").Font.Bold
= False

'Please note that you can not only
change the font of the rows but also
change the other properties like
alignment, font style, indentation,
border of the cells, color etc

'Alternative way to select the row
Worksheets(1).Rows(1).Font.Bold = False

'In below example we have change the
color of the border of rows 1,2 and 4 to
red
Set row124 = Union(Rows(1), Rows(2),
Rows(4))
row124.Borders.LineStyle = xlNone
row124.Borders.Color = vbRed

End Sub
```

5) Convert the data type of cell value

We can convert the given variable in any desired format. For example we we have a string as 09-jan-2013, we can convert it into date as mentioned below.

```
Sub conversion()
```

```
   date1 = CDate("09-jan-2013")
   MsgBox"Data type of date1 is"&
TypeName(date1)

'If the input to cdate function is not a
valid date, type mismatch error will
occur
'Similarly you can convert the string
into integer, float ect

   MsgBox CInt("243.6 ")

'To convert the number into string, you
can use cstr function

   no = 2344
   MsgBox CStr(no)

End Sub
```

6) Extract the part of cell value or string

you can use below functions to extract the part of the string

```
Sub extractString()

MsgBox Left("Lalu Prasad", 4)
 'get 4 characters from left side of
string
 'output - Lalu
 'Left function will get the specified
number of characters from left side of
the string

MsgBox Right("Lalu Prasad", 6)
```

```
'get 6 characters from the right side
of the string
'Right function will get the specified
number of characters from right side of
the string
'Output - Prasad

MsgBox Mid("Lalu Prasad", 6, 6)
'get 6 characters starting from index 6
'Mid function is used to get the fixed
length portion of string starting from
given position or index
'Output - Prasad

End Sub
```

7) Excel Macro to add leading zero to cell value

Excel Macro to add leading zero to any cell.

```
Sub addLeadingZero()

    'get the value from cell
    x = Sheet1.Cells(1, 1)
    'add leading zero

    x = "'000" & x

    'print value with zero
    MsgBox x

    'store value back in cell
    Sheet1.Cells(1, 1) = x

End Sub
```

7.3 Worksheet and Workbook

1) Select multiple ranges in a worksheet in excel macro

Below macro code shows how we can select multiple range like `A1:B8,C1:D8`

```
Sub select_multiple_range()

'We can select multiple range using
below code

Worksheets(1).Range("A1:B8,C1:D8").Font.
Bold = True


'In above code we have selected 2
ranges. First one is A1:B8 and other is
from C1:D8

'To access each range separately, we can
use below syntax

'In below code we have displayed the
total number of cells in first range
(area)

MsgBox
Worksheets(1).Range("A1:B8,C1:D8").Areas
(1).Cells.Count

End Sub
```

2) Clear the contents of entire worksheet in excel macro

```
Sub clear_worksheet_contents()

'We can select all cells from the given
sheet by using below code

Worksheets(1).Cells.Clear

'Above code will delete the data as well
as formatting from all cells from the
sheet1

End Sub
```

3) Access the worksheets by its index in excel macro

We can refer to the worksheets by it's index using below syntax. In below example we have used the sheet at index 1. Index of the leftmost worksheet is always 1 and it is incremented by 1 from left to right. We we move or add new worksheets in a workbook, the indices of the existing sheets also change.

```
Sub access_worksheets_by_index()

Worksheets(1).Select

End Sub
```

4) Access the worksheets by its name in excel macro

Below procedure will access the worksheets by its names. We can access the worksheets by its name by below syntax. In below example we have selected the sheet with the name balancesheet.

```
Sub access_worksheets_by_name()

Worksheets("balancesheet").Select

End Sub
```

This is how we can access the sheets using sheet name.

5) Delete multiple work sheets with excel macro

Below sub procedure will delete 2 sheets with name sheet2 and sheet3. We can select multiple worksheets by using below syntax.

```
Sub access_worksheets_by_name()

Worksheets("balancesheet").Select

'This is how we can access the sheets
using sheet name

End Sub
```

6) Add new workbook using excel macro

Below code will add new workbook and write some data into it and save it as well.

```
Sub Add_New_Workbook()

'We can add new workbook by using add
method of workbooks collection

Set new_workbook = Workbooks.Add

'access the cells in first sheet from
the newly added workbook
new_workbook.Worksheets(1).Cells(1, 1) =
"obama"

'save new workbook to hard disk
new_workbook.SaveAs "c:\temp.xlsx"

'close new workbook
new_workbook.Close

'release the memory of the object
associated with new_workbook
Set new_workbook = Nothing

End Sub
```

7) How to find out if particular Worksheet Exists Using Excel VBA Macro

Below Code/Example can be used to find if given worksheet exists in Workbook or not.

Macro Code to check if particular Worksheet Exists or Not in Workbook.

```
Dim mySheet
    mySheet = "Sagar"
    On Error Resume Next
    temp = Worksheets(mySheet ).Name
    If Err.Number = 0 Then
        MsgBox "Given Sheet Exists "
    Else
        Err.Clear
    MsgBox "Given Sheet Does not Exist"
End If
```

8) Access Sheets (Worksheets, Charts, Dialogs) Using Name/Index in Excel Macro

Below Example will show you how we can Access various sheets like worksheets, charts, modules, and dialog sheets using name in Macro.

Macro Code / Syntax -

```
Worksheets("Sheet1").Activate
Charts("Chart1").Activate
DialogSheets("Dialog1").Activate
```

In above code we are accessing the sheet1, chart1 and dialog1 using Excel Macro.

7.4 Files

1) Read data from text file

Excel macro to read a text file

```
Sub readFile()

Dim myfso As Scripting.FileSystemObject
Dim stream As Scripting.TextStream

Set myfso=New Scripting.FileSystemObject

'open text file in read mode.
Set stream=myfso.OpenTextFile
("c:\F1.txt", ForReading,True)

MsgBox stream.ReadAll

End Sub
```

2) Create text file

Please note that to perform file related functions in your project, you will have to add reference of microsoft script runtime. Here is the excel macro code to create a text file.

```
Sub createFile()

Dim myfso As Scripting.FileSystemObject

Dim stream As Scripting.TextStream

Set myfso=New Scripting.FileSystemObject
```

```
Set stream =
myfso.CreateTextFile("c:\F1.txt", True)

'Create text file at given path

stream.Write ("This is file creation
demo. if file exists, it will be
overwritten")

'Write data into opened file's stream

stream.Close

Set stream = Nothing

Set myfso = Nothing

End Sub
```

This is how You can create a file in excel macro.

3) Create and use dictionary object in excel macro

Please note that to use dictionary in your project, you will have to add reference of microsoft script runtime. Dictionary object allows you to store the elements in dynamic way using keys. Unlike arrays where values are stored using index, dictionary uses keys to store values.

```
Sub createDictionary()

Dim d1 As Scripting.Dictionary

'To add key in dictionary,use below code
Set d1 = New Scripting.Dictionary
d1.Add "sachin", 41
```

```
d1.Add "dhoni", 32

'To get the value at particular key
MsgBox d1.Item("sachin")

'to remove key from dictionary
d1.Remove "dhoni"

'To get all keys from the dictionary,
use below code
keyArray = d1.Keys


'to check if given key exists in the
dictionary

If d1.Exists("sachin") Then
    MsgBox "Key sachin exists"
Else
    MsgBox "Key sachin does not exist"
End If

'To remove all keys from dictionary, use
below code

d1.RemoveAll

End Sub
```

This is how you can use dictionary object in excel macro
You can store the values from 2 columns as key value pair
in dictionary.

7.5 Array in excel

1) Create and use array in excel macro

Arrays are used to store large number of elements in sequence. There are 2 types of Arrays in Excel Macro.

1.Fixed Size Array
2.Dynamic Array

```
Sub createArray()

Dim a(11)
a(0) = "sagar"
a(1) = 2
MsgBox a(1) & a(0)

'Or you can also create array like this
a=Array("sagar","amol","sachin",33,44,
55)
'*******Dynamic Array********
Dim b()

ReDim Preserve b(3)

'Above statement will resize the array
to size 4
'Preserve statement will keep the
existing values in the array intact

ReDim Preserve b(6)

'Again resize array to size of 7

End Sub
```

This is how we can array to store any number of values.

2) Filter Array

```
Sub Macro1()

    arr = Array("January", "February",
"March", "April", "May", "June", "July",
"August", "September", "October",
"November", "December")

    filt = Filter(arr, "J")

    For Each x In filt
        MsgBox (x)
    Next

End Sub
```

Output :- January
             June
             July

3) Join Array

```
Sub Macro1()

    arr = Array("Sunday","Monday",
"Tuesday","Wednesday","Thusday",
"Friday","Saturday")

    MsgBox (Join(arr))
```

```
End Sub
```

Output:- Sunday Monday Tuesday Wednesday Thusday
Friday Saturday

4) Ubound

```
Sub Macro1()

    arr = Array("Jan", "Feb", "Mar",
"Apr", "May", "Jun", "Jul", "Aug",
"Sep")
    MsgBox (LBound(arr))

    'Print Array Length
    MsgBox (UBound(arr))

End Sub
```

Output: 0
          8

7.6 Create modules in Excel Macro

Modules are used to store the related procedures and
functions

1.Modules contain the functions that provide unique
functionality
2.We can group similar functions and procedures in
separate module
3.Class module contains properties and methods of that
particular class
4.For example - we can create a student class which can be
used to store/retrieve student properties like student
name, student id, student address etc.

7.7 How to pause the execution of Macro in Excel

In below example, you will see how we can pause the execution of macro before executing next statement. Please note that wscript is not available in Excel VBA Macro. It is available only in vbscript.

Code and Syntax for making the programm wait in Excel VBA is given below.

```
a = 10

Application.Wait(Now()+TimeValue("0:00:11"))

msgbox a
```

As you can see in above code, I have used Application.Wait statement.
if you execute this code, you will see that value in a is prompted after 11 seconds.

To wait for say 10 mins, you will have to use below code

```
a = 10

Application.Wait(Now()+TimeValue("0:10:00"))

msgbox a
```

So here the format of TimeValue is -

TimeValue("hh:mm:ss")) - So you can give any value in hour/minute/second to make macro wait for that particular time.

7.8 List of commonly used Excel functions

I am using Excel Macros since last few years and from that experience I have created the list of commonly used excel functions that we can use.

Formula	Value	Description
=ABS(-11)	11	gets Absolute value
=ADDRESS(1,1)	$B$1	gets the address of cell
=AGGREGATE(4,0,A1:A10)	33	Calculates aggregates
=BIN2DEC(101)	5	converst binary to decimal
=CELL("contents",A1)	33	gets the contents of given cell
=CHAR(65)	A	gets the character for ascii value
=CHOOSE(2,33,44)	44	selects nth value from the given set of values
=CONVERT(23,"m","ft")	75.45 93175 9	Converts the number in different measurement

		units
=COUNT(A1,B3)	1	counts the number of cells having numbers in it
=COUNTA(A1:A7)	7	counts non empty cells
=COUNTIF(A1:A7,2)	0	counts the cells that meet the condition
=EXACT("sagar","sagar")	TRUE	checks if two string are similar or not
=FACT(5)	120	gets the factorial of the number
=FIND("ten","sachin tendulkar")	8	finds the position of given string in other string
=FIXED(19.434,2)	19.43	rounds the number
=FLOOR(45345.6756,1)	45345	gets the integer number
=CEILING(45345.676,1)	45346	gets the integer number
=NOW()	25-10-2013 17:19	gets current time
=DAY(now())	25	gets current day
=GCD(6,8)	2	find GCD
=HLOOKUP(2,A1:A10,3)	#N/A	Horizontal Lookup
=VLOOKUP(2,A1:A10,3)	#N/A	Vertical Lookup
=HOUR(NOW())	17	gets current hour
=HYPERLINK("http://www.google.com","goog")	goog	creates the hyperlink in the cell

=IF(12>10,"12 is big","12 not big")	12 is big	executes conditional statements
=INT(323.55)	323	gets the integer part of the number
=ISBLANK(a55)	TRUE	checks if the given cell value is blank
=ISEVEN(22)	TRUE	checks if the given value is even
=ISNONTEXT(a55)	TRUE	checks if the givenvalue is non-text
=ISNUMBER(22.44)	TRUE	checks if the given value is number
=ISODD(34)	FALSE	checks if the given value is odd
=ISTEXT("dsdsd")	TRUE	checks if the givenvalue is a text
=LARGE(A1:A44,1)	56	gets the nth largest value from the given set
=LCM(6,8)	24	gets the Least Common Multiple
=LEFT("sachin tendulkar",6)	sachin	gets the n characters from the left side of the string
=LEN("sachin")	6	gets the length of the given value
=LOWER("Sagar Salunke")	sagar salunk e	converts the value into lower case
=MATCH(33,A1:A77,0)	1	searches the value in given range

=MAX(A1:A44)	56	finds the max value from given range
=Min(A1:A44)	3	finds the min value from given range
=MONTH(now())	10	gets the current month
=MOD(44,3)	2	gets the remainder of division
=MID("sachin tendulkar",7,33)	tendu lkar	gets the n characters from the given string
=MINUTE(now())	19	gets current minutes
=NETWORKDAYS("20-jan-2013",NOW())	200	counts the weekdays from given dates
=OR(12>33,FALSE)	FALSE	checks the OR conditions
=POWER(2,2)	4	gets the power of given number
=PROPER("sagar salunke")	Sagar Salunk e	Converst the first letter of word to upper case
=QUOTIENT(5,2)	2	gets the QUOTIENT
=RAND()	0.988 17193 5	gets the random number betweem 0 and 1
=RANDBETWEEN(1,100)	35	gets the random number between 1 and 100
=REPLACE("sachin	sachin	replace the part of

ten",8,3,"Anjali")	Anjalie n	string by other string
=RIGHT("sagar salunke",8)	salun ke	get n characters from the right side of the string
=ROUND(4545.67,1)	4545. 7	rounds the number
=ROW(A1)	3	gets the row number of given cell
=SEARCH("ten","sachin tendulkar")	8	search one string in other
=SMALL(A1:A99,2)	5	gets the nth smallest number from the given set
=SQRT(4)	2	gets the square root of the number
=SUBSTITUTE("sagar salunke","sagar","ganesh")	ganes h salunk e	replace the part of string by other string
=SUM(A1:A11)	268	gets the sum of given numbers
=SUMIF(A1:A10,33)	231	gets the sum of numbers if criteria is fulfilled
=TODAY()	25-10-2013	gets today's date
=TRIM(" sagar salunke ")	sagar salunk e	removes the spaces from left and right side
=TYPE(22)	1	gets the data type of the parameter
=TRUNC(3434.56767)	3434.	truncates the

	56	number
=UPPER("sagar salunke")	SAGAR SALUNKE	converts the letters to upper case
=WEEKDAY(NOW())	6	gets the weekday from the given date
=YEAR(NOW())	2013	gets the year from the given date

7.9 Get the month name of given date

```
Sub getMonthName()

  'Print current month name

  MsgBox MonthName(Month(Now))

  'To print month name of any given date
you can use below macro ccde

  MsgBox MonthName(Month("09-jan-1988"))

End Sub
```

7.10 Get the stock data from yahoo finance

Below procedure can be used to get the stock information from yahoo finance.

```
Sub getYahooFinance()
```

```
'Below script will download the quotes
for given symbol from yahoo finance
'more info at ->
http://www.jarloo.com/yahoo_finance/

'qURL =
"http://finance.yahoo.com/d/quotes.csv?s
=AAPL+GOOG+MSFT&f=nv"
'http://finance.yahoo.com/d/quotes.csv?s
=AAPL+GOOG+MSFT&f=nv

qURL =
"http://ichart.finance.yahoo.com/table.c
sv?s=rcom.BO&ignore=.csv"
With
Sheet1.QueryTables.Add(Connection:="URL;
"&qURL,
Destination:=Sheet1.Range("A1"))

    .BackgroundQuery = True
    .TablesOnlyFromHTML = False
    .Refresh BackgroundQuery:=False
    .SaveData = True
End With

End Sub
```

7.11 Get stock finance data from Google NSE BSE

Below program will get stock/finance information in xml
format from google finance.
You can give the stocks from NSE and BSE as well.

```
'Specify the url to connect to
```

```
URL="http://www.google.com/ig/api?stock=
rcom"
Set objHTTP=CreateObject
("MSXML2.XMLHTTP")

Call objHTTP.Open("GET", URL, False)
objHTTP.Send

'The response comes in the form of xml
stream.

MsgBox (objHTTP.ResponseText)
```

7.12 Excel Macro to process xml file

```
Sub processXML()

Set xDoc =
CreateObject("MSXML2.DOMDocument")

'to load the xml string
'xDoc.LoadXML
("<book><str>hello</str></book>")
'to load xml from file, use below syntax

xDoc.Load ("c:\abc.xml")
'Display all elements and their values
Call DisplayNode(xDoc.ChildNodes, 0)

MsgBox str1

'We can also use xpath to get the
collection of nodes
```

```
xDoc.setProperty "SelectionLanguage",
"XPath"

strPath = "//book"

Set nodelist =
xDoc.DocumentElement.SelectNodes(strPath
)

MsgBox "No of Nodes Found by using xpath
is -> " & nodelist.Length & " Node"

Set xDoc = Nothing

End Sub
```

Recursive function to traverse all the nodes inside xml file/ String

```
Public Sub DisplayNode(ByRef Nodes,
ByVal Indent)

  Dim xNode
  Indent = Indent + 2

For Each xNode In Nodes

 If xNode.NodeType = NODE_TEXT Then

    str1 = str1 & " " &
xNode.ParentNode.nodeName & ":" &
xNode.NodeValue

End If
```

```
If xNode.HasChildNodes Then

    DisplayNode xNode.ChildNodes, Indent

 End If

Next

End Sub
```

7.13 Display a dialog box

We can display message box / dialog box with yes/no buttons in excel macro using msgbox function

```
Sub messageBox()

ret = MsgBox("Yes - No Buttons",
vbYesNoCancel, "MessageBox Macro")
'Please note that second parameter in
the function msgbox decided which
buttons to display on the dialog 'box.

If ret = 6 Then
    MsgBox "You cliked on Yes"
ElseIf ret = 7 Then
    MsgBox "You cliked on No"
Else
    'ret = 2
  MsgBox "You cliked on Cancel"
End If

End Sub
```

7.14 Macro to calculate system idle time in Excel.

In below example, I have shown how we can find the system idle time using excel vba macro.

Code and Syntax to calculate system idle time.
In below code, GetIdleTime() function returns the number of seconds the system has been idle for.
Here idle means that there is no input from user from keyboard or mouse.

```vba
Private Type LASTINPUTINFO
   cbSize As Long
   dwTime As Long
End Type

'*********************************

Private Declare Sub GetLastInputInfo Lib
"user32" (ByRef plii As LASTINPUTINFO)
Private Declare Function GetTickCount
Lib "kernel32" () As Long

'*********************************

Function GetIdleTime() As Single
  Dim a As LASTINPUTINFO
  a.cbSize = LenB(a)
  GetLastInputInfo a
```

```
    GetIdleTime= (GetTickCount - a.dwTime)
/ 1000
End Function


'* * * * * * * * * * * * * * * * * * * * * * * * * * * * * * * *


Sub check()
        Application.Wait (Now() +
TimeValue("0:00:11"))
    ' make the system idle for 11 sec.
Donot type from keyboard or click from
mouse
        MsgBox getIdleTime()
End Sub
```

LASTINPUTINFO is a structure defined by microsoft and it Contains the time of the last input.

GetTickCount functions gets the number of milliseconds that have elapsed since the system was started, up to 49.7 days.

When you will execute above programm, you will be prompted approx. 11 as system idle time

8. Automating Charts using Excel Macro

In this chapter you will learn about how to generate charts and format them using excel macros.

8.1. Create a chart

Suppose you want to create a graph for below data.

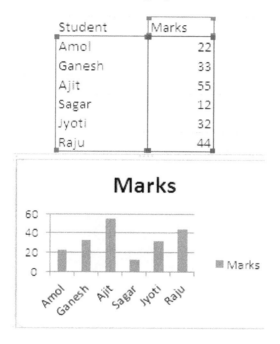

Figure 23 - Create a Chart using Macro

Below macro code can be used to create a chart. In the first line, We have set the chart type to `xlColumnClustered`. Other chart types that we can create in Excel 2010 are

1. Column charts (We are using this one)
2. Line charts

3. Pie charts
4. Bar charts
5. Area charts
6. XY (scatter) charts
7. Stock charts
8. Surface charts
9. Doughnut charts
10. Bubble charts
11. Radar charts

```
'create a clustered column chart

ActiveSheet.Shapes.AddChart.Select
    ActiveChart.ChartType =
xlColumnClustered

'Set the source data for chart

    ActiveChart.SetSourceData
Source:=Range("Sheet1!$B$6:$C$12")

'Format the data series of the chart

ActiveChart.SeriesCollection(1).Select

    With Selection.Format.Fill
        .Visible = msoTrue
        .ForeColor.ObjectThemeColor =
msoThemeColorAccent1
        .ForeColor.TintAndShade = 0
        .ForeColor.Brightness = 0
        .Solid
    End With
```

```
    With Selection.Format.Fill
        .Visible = msoTrue
        .ForeColor.ObjectThemeColor =
msoThemeColorAccent3
        .ForeColor.TintAndShade = 0
        .ForeColor.Brightness = -0.25
        .Transparency = 0
        .Solid
    End With

'Format the plot area of the chart

    ActiveChart.PlotArea.Select
    With Selection.Format.Fill
        .Visible = msoTrue
        .ForeColor.ObjectThemeColor =
msoThemeColorAccent3
        .ForeColor.TintAndShade = 0
        .ForeColor.Brightness = -0.25
        .Solid
    End With
    With Selection.Format.Fill
        .Visible = msoTrue
        .ForeColor.ObjectThemeColor =
msoThemeColorAccent5
        .ForeColor.TintAndShade = 0
        .ForeColor.Brightness =
0.8000000119
        .Transparency = 0
        .Solid
    End With
```

1. Create a pivot table.

2. Create pivot chart.

8.2 Create a pivot table

Consider below data in excel sheet. Now we are going to create a pivot table from this data with macro.

⊿	A	B	C	D
1	Order Id	Order Amount	City	Order Date
2	2	345	Pune	21-Feb-14
3	3	5645	Mumbai	21-Feb-14
4	43	23	Pune	22-Feb-14
5	4	435	Pune	23-Feb-14
6	23	5646	Chennai	21-Feb-14
7	5	6765	Banglore	21-Feb-14
8	22	234	New York	21-Feb-14
9	214	4545	CA	24-Feb-14
10	545	323	CA	21-Feb-14
11	6	2323	TX	24-Feb-14
12	33	4545	TX	21-Feb-14

Figure 24- Source Data for the Pivot table

Here is the macro for creating the pivot table.

```
'add new pivot table.
'Note that we have provided source data
'and destination for the table

Range("A1:D12").Select
ActiveWorkbook.PivotCaches.Create(Source
Type:=xlDatabase, SourceData:= _
```

```
                "Sheet1!R1C1:R12C4",
Version:=xlPivotTableVersion14).CreatePi
votTable _
          TableDestination:="Sheet1!R2C6",
TableName:="PivotTable5", DefaultVersion
_
          :=xlPivotTableVersion14

    Sheets("Sheet1").Select
    Cells(2, 6).Select
'here we have added data fields

ActiveSheet.PivotTables("PivotTable5").A
ddDataField ActiveSheet.PivotTables( _

"PivotTable5").PivotFields("Order
Amount"), "Sum of Order Amount", xlSum

'here we have set the orientation of the
table

    With
ActiveSheet.PivotTables("PivotTable5").P
ivotFields("City")
          .Orientation = xlRowField
          .Position = 1
    End With
```

After you run above macro, you will see below pivot table created in the same worksheet. As you can see, pivottable gives you idea about the data. From below table, we can easily find out how much amount of sales have done in given city.

Row Labels ▼	Sum of Order Amount
Banglore	6765
CA	4868
Chennai	5646
Mumbai	5645
New York	234
Pune	803
TX	6868
Grand Total	30829

Figure 25 - Pivot Table

8.3 Create a pivot chart

Now let us create the pivot chart from the given Pivot table.

To create the pivot char, again we can use macro. We have to give the source data for the pivot chart similar to how we do with pivot table. After that we can create a pivot chart very easily. Actually when you add a pivot chart, Excel first creates the Pivot table and from that table, it creates the chart.

```
ActiveWorkbook.PivotCaches.Create(Source
Type:=xlDatabase, SourceData:= _
      "Sheet1!R2C6:R10C7",
Version:=xlPivotTableVersion14).CreatePi
votTable _
```

```
TableDestination:="Sheet1!R14C6",
TableName:="PivotTable7", DefaultVersion
_
        :=xlPivotTableVersion14
    Sheets("Sheet1").Select
    Cells(14, 6).Select

    'add chart
    ActiveSheet.Shapes.AddChart().Select
    ActiveChart.ChartType =
xlColumnClustered
    ActiveChart.SetSourceData
Source:=Range("Sheet1!$F$14:$H$31")
    With
ActiveSheet.PivotTables("PivotTable7").P
ivotFields("Row Labels")
        .Orientation = xlRowField
        .Position = 1
    End With


'add the data fields for the pivot table

ActiveSheet.PivotTables("PivotTable7").A
ddDataField ActiveSheet.PivotTables( _
        "PivotTable7").PivotFields("Sum
of Order Amount"), "Sum of Sum of Order
Amount" _
        , xlSum


ActiveChart.SeriesCollection(1).Select
    With
ActiveSheet.PivotTables("PivotTable7").P
ivotFields("Row Labels")
        .PivotItems("Grand
Total").Visible = False
    End With
```

```
ActiveSheet.ChartObjects(1).Activate
```

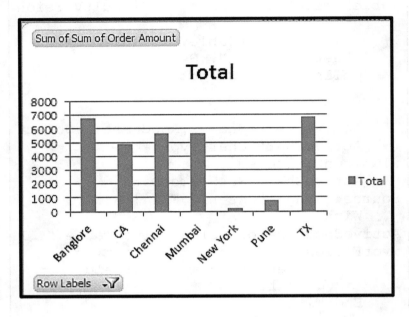

Figure 26 - PivotChart

9. Working with other office products

In this chapter you will learn about how you can communicate with other office products like...

1. Sending an email from outlook.
2. Working with Microsoft access database.

9.1 Send mail with attachment

Below Excel Macro Example will send the email from outlook with attachment. You can attach any file like ,xls, .pdf etc.

You can also send an email based on cell value. For example - if cell value is Yes, Then it will send an email. The email is sent automatically provided that your email client outlook is configured correctly.

Please note that this macro cannot be used to send an email from lotus notes.

You can send an email to multiple addresses/recipients by just editing the TO property of mail item object in below example.

Excel Macro Code to send an email from outloo is given below. We have also added the attachment in the form of word document located at C:\my.doc

```
Set Outlook =
CreateObject("Outlook.Application")

Set Message = Outlook.CreateItem(0)

With Message
        .Subject = "Any Subject "
        .HTMLBody = "Any TextBody "
        .Recipients.Add ("abc@gmail.com")
End With

Set myAttachments = Message.Attachments

myAttachments.Add "C:\my.doc",1, 1, "my"

Message.Display

Message.Send
```

Above program will send an email to abc@gmail.com with my.doc attached to it.

Please note that to send the workbook as attachment, it can be done very easily with below ine of code

ActiveWorkbook.SendMail "sagar.salunke@gmail.com"

Please note that before you run above macro, your outlook client should have been configured correctly.

9.2 Reading data from Microsoft Access database

We can read data from any external application or database using ADODB in excel macro. In below example, we have connected to the access database stored at – G:\priyanka\vb6\admission_project.mdb

After connection is made, we have fired select sql query to read all records from the table called Course. Then using a for loop, we have shown the data from each record.

```
Set db =
createobject("ADODB.Connection")

db.Open
"Provider=Microsoft.Jet.OLEDB.4.0;Data
Source=G:\priyanka\vb6\admission_project
.mdb;Persist Security Info=False"

Set rst =
createobject("ADODB.Recordset")

rst.Open "select * from Course ", db,3

id = rst.RecordCount

For i=0 to id-1
 msgbox rst.fields(0) & rst.fields(1) &
rst.fields(2) & rst.fields(3)
rst.Movenext
Next
```

www.ingramcontent.com/pod-product-compliance
Lightning Source LLC
Chambersburg PA
CBHW060945050326
40689CB00012B/2569